GREAT MINDS OF SCIENCE

Niels Bohr
Physicist and Humanitarian

Naomi Pasachoff

Enslow Publishers, Inc.

40 Industrial Road   PO Box 38
Box 398   Aldershot
Berkeley Heights, NJ 07922   Hants GU12 6BP
USA   UK
http://www.enslow.com

*To my husband, Jay, whose dedication to physical science has been
an inspiration and whose loving support has been my mainstay.*

Library of Congress Cataloging-in-Publication Data

Pasachoff, Naomi E.
  Niels Bohr : physicist and humanitarian / Naomi Pasachoff.
    p. cm. — (Great minds of science)
Summary: A biography of the Danish physicist who won a Nobel Prize for
his discoveries about the nature of the atom, saved thousands of Jews
from the Nazis, and, after helping to develop the atomic bomb,
campaigned for peaceful uses of atomic energy.
Includes bibliographical references and index.
Contents: A secret message — Growing up in Denmark — Postdoctoral work
in England — Groundbreaking work — A world-class institute — The
winds of war — An open world.
  ISBN 0-7660-1997-7
  1. Bohr, Niels Henrik David, 1885–1962—Juvenile literature. 2.
Physicists—Denmark—Biography—Juvenile literature. [1. Bohr, Niels
Henrik David, 1885–1962. 2. Physicists. 3. Nobel Prizes—Biography.] I.
Title. II. Series.
QC16.B63 P37 2003
530'.092—dc21

                              2002003887

Printed in the United States of America

10 9 8 7 6 5 4 3

To Our Readers:
We have done our best to make sure all Internet Addresses in this book were active and
appropriate when we went to press. However, the author and the publisher have no control
over and assume no liability for the material available on those Internet sites or on other
Web sites they may link to. Any comments or suggestions can be sent by e-mail to
comments@enslow.com or to the address on the back cover.

Illustration Credits: Courtesy of Jay M. Pasachoff, pp. 41, 61, 66, 69, 72, 100,
104; David Torsiello/Enslow Publishers, Inc., p. 107, Susan Rosnowski/Enslow
Publishers, Inc., pp. 111, 112; Enslow Publishers, Inc., pp. 21, 31, 47, 83;
National Archives, pp. 95, 76; Nature, courtesy AIP Emilio Segrè Visual
Archives, p. 29; Niels Bohr Archive, courtesy AIP Emilio Segrè Visual Archives,
Margrethe Bohr Collection, p. 10; Niels Bohr Archive, courtesy AIP Emilio
Segrè Visual Archives, pp. 17, 19; Photo by Mark Oliphant, AIP Emilio Segrè
Visual Archives, Margrethe Bohr Collection, p. 37; Photograph by P. Ehrenfest
Jr., courtesy AIP Emilio Segrè Visual Archives, Weisskopf Collection, p. 50;
Photograph by Paul Ehrenfest, courtesy AIP Emilio Segrè Visual Archives, p. 53.

Cover Illustration: Getty Images (background); AIP Emilio Segrè Visual
Archives, Weber Collection (inset).

Contents

Acknowledgments

A NUMBER OF INDIVIDUALS WERE KIND enough to take the time to read through a draft of this book and to make valuable comments. I wish to thank my husband, Professor Jay M. Pasachoff, of Williams College; my daughters, Eloise and Deborah; Agnete Kalckar of Massachusetts, whose husband was a colleague of Bohr; Professor Marek Demianski, of the Copernicus Astronomical Observatory and Williams College; Dr. George Rybicki of the Harvard-Smithsonian Center for Astrophysics; and Dr. Spencer Weart, of the American Institute of Physics. I would also like to thank Dr. Finn Aaserud and Felicity Pors of the Niels Bohr Archives in Copenhagen for their hospitality and assistance. Any errors that may remain in the book, however, are my responsibility alone.

A Secret Message

THE TIME WAS EARLY 1943. THE SECOND World War was in its fourth year. Much of Europe was controlled by Hitler and his Nazis. The place was the House of Honor in Copenhagen, capital of Denmark. Technically a neutral country, Denmark had actually been under the thumb of the Nazis for nearly three years.

The splendid House of Honor had originally been home to the owner of Denmark's Carlsberg brewery. In his will, the wealthy brewer had arranged for it to become the residence for life of Denmark's greatest citizen. For more than ten years, physicist Niels Bohr and his family had lived there.

Bohr entertained many distinguished visitors at the House of Honor. Among them were monarchs, heads of state, and fellow scientists. Today's visitor, however, was a member of the Danish underground resistance movement against the Nazis. Out of earshot of the hidden microphones planted by the Nazis, the visitor explained that Bohr would soon receive a set of keys from England. Tiny holes had been drilled into two of the keys. Inside each, the same important message would be compressed into a microdot—a photograph reduced to the size of a printed period. The visitor asked Bohr if he would like him to remove the microdots and enlarge the message when the keys arrived. Bohr gratefully accepted the offer.

After the tiny pieces of microfilm were studied under a microscope, they revealed a letter from British physicist James Chadwick. Bohr had known Chadwick since 1912, when they both worked at the same laboratory in Manchester, England. Chadwick's letter urged Bohr to come to England: "There is no scientist in the world who would be more acceptable both to our university people and to the general public. . . . I have in mind a particular problem in which your assistance would be of the greatest help."[1]

Like a secret agent, Bohr sent his reply back by the same route. He wrote, "I feel it to be my duty in our desperate situation to help resist the threat against the freedom of our institutions and to assist in the protection of the exiled scientists who have sought refuge here."[2] He added, however, that the time might come when he might change his mind.

The "problem" Chadwick had in mind involved a top secret project. It was called the Manhattan Project. It was started by the United States government in 1942. The goal of the project was to produce the first atomic bomb. By late 1943, England sent its own team of scientists to the U.S. to help with the work. Both England and the U.S. feared that the Nazis might have been developing their own atomic bomb. If they were to succeed in developing the bomb first, Germany would surely conquer the world. Many scientists thought it was dangerous for any nation to have atomic weapons, but they feared

Niels Bohr and his wife, Margrethe, sit outside the Carlsberg House of Honor in Copenhagen, Denmark.

the Nazis even more. Since Niels Bohr was a pioneer in understanding the atom, he could have greatly aided the Manhattan Project. Eventually, in December 1943, he did join the Project.

In addition to his work with the atom, Bohr also added a great deal to the development of quantum theory, a branch of physics. Quantum theory is a cornerstone of modern science. Bohr's work in quantum theory eventually helped lead to many devices like lasers and transistors. There is no question that Niels Bohr stands as one of the greatest scientific minds of all time. But his contributions to history are not limited to science alone.

Bohr always promoted cooperation among all countries of the world. He believed that the free exchange of ideas between nations was an important part of maintaining peace. Also, while in Denmark in the midst of World War II, Bohr worked tirelessly to save thousands of Jewish refugees from the Nazis. And after helping to develop the atomic bomb, he campaigned for peaceful uses of atomic energy. In 1950, he wrote a letter to the United Nations that argued for rational atomic policies. In 1957, Bohr was awarded the first U.S. Atoms for Peace Award.

Niels Bohr was more than a scientific genius. He was also a humanitarian and champion of peace.

Growing Up in Denmark

NIELS HENRIK DAVID BOHR WAS BORN IN Copenhagen on October 7, 1885. His father, Christian Bohr, was a professor of physiology (the study of how living things function) at the University of Copenhagen. His mother, Ellen Adler Bohr, came from a Jewish family involved in banking, politics, and education. Worried that her three children—Jenny, Niels, and Harald— might be discriminated against as Jews, Ellen Bohr had them baptized as Christians in 1891. As a teenager, Niels went through a brief but intense period of religious commitment. However, he formally left the Lutheran church before his marriage in 1912.

Niels's closest lifelong friend was his younger brother, Harald. Harald became a distinguished mathematician. Both boys were deeply influenced by their father. During walks and outings, Christian Bohr pointed out the wonders of nature to his sons. He read masterpieces of literature aloud to them. His favorite writers were the German poet Goethe, the English playwright Shakespeare, and the English novelist Dickens.

Christian Bohr was a member of the Royal Danish Academy of Sciences and Letters. Other members included philosopher Harald Høffding, physicist Christian Christiansen, and philologist (a scientist of language) Vilhelm Thomsen. These men met regularly in each others' homes for lively conversations. Harald and Niels were allowed to sit in on these meetings in the Bohr home. From these sessions, Niels learned the value of intense conversation and sharing ideas.

Christian Bohr was also a sports fan. The founder of Copenhagen's university soccer club, he trained his boys to play soccer. In 1908, Harald won a silver medal for Denmark as halfback on its Olympic soccer team. Niels also played soccer, but never as successfully as his brother.

Niels was a strong student at the Gammelholm School. He attended the school from age seven until he entered the University of Copenhagen in 1903. He did well in every subject except Danish composition. Throughout his life, Bohr wrestled with words to make them convey his precise meaning. He would always have trouble committing his thoughts to writing. He wrote many drafts, even of personal letters. His writing problem was worsened by his poor handwriting. As often as possible, he would dictate his work to someone else, who would copy it down. At first, family members filled this role. Later, a series of younger scientists would act as scribes. These assistants helped Bohr refine his thinking by discussing his ideas with him.

A school assignment Niels tackled at age eleven revealed his passion for accuracy. Instructed to draw a specific house with its fenced garden, Niels first counted all of the fence pickets before picking up his pencil.

By the time Niels began studying high school

math and physics, his abilities could not be missed. Since he read the current scientific journals, he began to notice statements that were wrong or outdated in his textbooks. A classmate once asked him what he would do if faced with an exam question on one of these statements. Niels answered without hesitation: "Tell them, of course, how things really are."[1]

At the university, Niels Bohr studied physics with Christiansen and philosophy with Høffding. Just as these professors participated with Niels's father in an informal discussion group, Niels and Harald participated in a student discussion group. Members of this student group noted how Harald and Niels were able to complete each other's thoughts. Niels was known as the soft-spoken brother. He was often urged to speak louder.

Another pair of brothers, the Nørlunds, also participated in this student group. It was through them that Niels Bohr first met Margrethe Nørlund, their sister, in 1909. Niels and Margrethe would eventually marry in 1912.

In 1905, each of the physics students was

Niels Bohr and his mother, Ellen, pictured some time around 1902.

required to deliver a lecture. This lecture could be on a subject of his choosing. Twenty-year-old Niels Bohr delivered a lecture on radioactivity. At the time, radioactivity was still a relatively new field. In the laboratories of Marie Curie and others, mysterious rays promised to reveal new truths about radioactivity and the atom. Bohr would later go on to make significant contributions of his own in the study of the atom. His student presentation, however, contributed no new insights to the science of radioactivity. But like all his work, it was very thorough.

Niels Bohr was destined to make his name as a theoretical physicist. However, in 1905, he won a gold medal from the Royal Danish Academy of Sciences and Letters for his experimental work. Bohr's prize-winning experiment involved the surface tension of water.[2] (Surface tension makes the surface of a liquid act like a stretched elastic sheet. For example, an insect can stand on a pond's surface because of surface tension.) About thirty years later, Bohr was able to draw on this experimental knowledge to develop a theory about the atomic nucleus—the positively charged core of an atom. This "liquid drop" theory would later help unlock the mystery of atomic energy.

After Bohr completed his undergraduate degree in 1907, he went on for a master's degree and then a doctorate in physics. For both degrees, he studied and wrote about the electron theory of metals. The electron—a negatively charged particle—had been discovered only ten years earlier by Sir Joseph John Thomson (known to everyone as J.J.). Thomson was head of the Cavendish Laboratory at the University of

Niels Bohr (right) and his younger brother, Harald, pictured in 1934.

Cambridge in England. Thomson's discovery of the electron was one of the first indications that atoms were not the smallest particles. (The word atom comes from ancient Greek. It means "that which cannot be further cut.") In Thomson's model of the atom, negative electrons circled in rings within a thin fog of positively charged material.

Scientists already knew that metals like iron, tin, and gold were elements. That means they could not be broken down into other substances by heat, light, or electricity. In the early 1800s, another Englishman, John Dalton, had suggested that a different type of atom makes up each element.

Scientists also knew that metals, like other elements, had characteristic properties. For example, metals are shiny. They are good conductors of heat and electricity. Some, such as iron, are attracted by magnets. For his graduate degrees, Bohr did mathematical calculations that related electron theory to the properties of metals. According to the electron theory, the characteristic properties of metals came from the movement and collisions of electrons traveling between their atoms.

After writing at least "fourteen more or less divergent rough drafts" of his doctoral thesis, Bohr finally received his doctorate in spring 1911.[3] Sadly, Niels's father, Christian Bohr, had died earlier that same year. Niels Bohr dedicated his thesis "in deepest gratitude to the

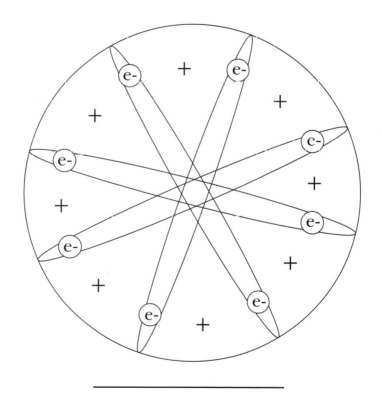

J.J. Thomson's model of the atom had negatively charged electrons circling in rings within a thin fog of positively charged material.

memory of my father."[4] The thesis concluded that the electron theory of metals failed to explain their magnetic properties. Professor Christiansen regretted that the thesis had not been published in a foreign language: "Here in Denmark there was hardly anybody well informed enough about the electron theory of metals to be able to judge a thesis on this subject."[5]

Before Christian Bohr's death, he had arranged for his son Niels to get a grant from the Carlsberg Foundation. This grant allowed Niels Bohr to go to England to study with J.J. Thomson. While researching his thesis, Bohr had discovered some serious errors in Thomson's work on electrons. He looked forward to discussing these errors with Thomson himself.

Postdoctoral Work in England

MANY YEARS LATER, BOHR REMEMBERED how much he looked forward to going to the Cavendish: "I considered first of all Cambridge as the center of physics, and Thomson was a most wonderful man . . . , a genius who showed the way for everybody."[1] Bohr was not the only person to have such a good opinion of J.J. Thomson. When the nearly twenty-six-year-old Dane arrived in Cambridge in autumn 1911, both Thomson and the laboratory he headed were highly esteemed by the physics community. Thomson was only fifty-five years old but had been director of the Cavendish for twenty-seven years. In 1906, he had been awarded the Nobel Prize for physics for his work on the electron.

Bohr arrived in England with a copy of his thesis, translated into poor English by a Copenhagen neighbor. Although the neighbor had spent some time in England, he knew little physics. Bohr's English was imperfect. Years later, Bohr laughed at himself for translating the Danish term for "electrical charge" into the English words "electrical loading." Untroubled by such thoughts at the time, he hoped Thomson would help him get the thesis published in English. Bohr also hoped to discuss the errors he had found in Thomson's work on electron theory.

Bohr's early letters home revealed his high hopes for his stay in Cambridge. He wrote to his fiancée, Margrethe, enthusiastically: "After my arrival the first thing I did was to pay my respects to Thomson. He was extremely pleasant, and we had a little talk during which he said he would be interested in seeing my treatise. . . . You can imagine how happy I was when I left. . . . I am so anxious to learn what he will think of the whole thing and also of all the criticism."[2]

A few days later he wrote his brother, Harald: "Things are going so well for me. . . . I have just been talking to J.J. Thomson and explained to him as well as I could my ideas. . . . If only you knew what it meant to me to speak to such a man."[3] Bohr went on to tell Harald that Thomson had invited him to Sunday dinner at Trinity College. Apparently Bohr believed that Thomson would read the translated thesis by that time and would discuss it with him.

An early letter to his mother, however, indicated that Bohr had some trouble adjusting to his new life abroad. "But you must not think that everything is going all that smoothly. You have no idea of the confusion reigning in the Cavendish laboratory, and a poor foreigner, who does not even know what the different things that he cannot find are called, is in a very awkward position."[4]

Bohr soon realized that his Cambridge experience would not work out as he had hoped. Looking back years later on what went wrong, he blamed himself for starting off on the wrong foot with Thomson: "It was a disappointment that

Thomson was not interested to learn that his calculations were not correct. That was . . . my fault. I had no great knowledge of English, and there I did not know how to express myself. And I could only say this is incorrect. And he was not interested in the accusation that it was not correct, and so on."[5]

Another factor in Thomson's lack of interest in Bohr is that he had left electron theory behind him. He was now working on what he called "rays of positive electricity."[6] Thomson assigned Bohr an experiment on positive rays, which Bohr thought a waste of time. "There was absolutely nothing to be gotten out of it," Bohr said.[7]

A further source of disappointment was his failure to get his thesis published. Here Thomson was not at fault. After a young physicist helped Bohr improve the English, Thomson forwarded the thesis to the Cambridge Philosophical Society for publication in its journal. In May 1912, the society informed Bohr that the thesis would be publishable only if cut in half. Bohr briefly considered and then rejected the suggestion. His carefully constructed arguments, he insisted, could not be expressed in half the length. Bohr's doctoral thesis would not be published in English until 1972. Had it been published earlier, it might have made a major contribution to the development of physics.

Although many years later he recalled feeling "rather unhappy in Cambridge,"[8] Bohr did enjoy certain aspects of life there. The stately university town charmed him. He greatly admired the scientists he met. He had time not only for a lot of reading but also for working on his English language skills. At the end of his life he remembered reading Charles Dickens's *Pickwick Papers* as "a way to get into English." He "looked up every word" of whose exact translation into Danish he was uncertain, even if he could figure out what it meant.[9] He kept the red dictionary he bought for that purpose for the rest of his life. He relied on it even while writing his final papers.

While Bohr regretted having "no friends among the younger students," he did have a social life in Cambridge.[10] Friends and former students of his father's were hospitable to him and offered him advice. It was not unusual for a foreign student with his own means of support to spend a year abroad working under different senior scientists. One of his father's friends suggested that Bohr think about transferring to Ernest Rutherford's laboratory in Manchester, England. It was an inspired suggestion.

New Zealand-born Ernest Rutherford was also a Nobel laureate. Rutherford was a physicist, but his 1908 award was for chemistry, "for his investigations of radioactive elements and the chemistry of radioactive substances."[11] Rutherford may be unique in that the most important discovery of his life came after his Nobel. Earlier in 1911, while Bohr was still in Denmark, Rutherford announced his discovery of a small, positively charged object within the atom. Nearly all the mass of an atom is concentrated in this object, called the nucleus. Rutherford's discovery led him to propose his own model of the atom. This model was similar to a miniature solar system. The nucleus at the center of the atom held the atom's positive

Ernest Rutherford (above) would have a tremendous influence on the life and work of Niels Bohr.

charge and stood in for the sun. Electrons were imagined traveling around the nucleus in circles, like planets.

There was a problem with Rutherford's model of the atom, however. According to the laws of physics, the electrons should have been giving off energy as they moved. While spending their energy, they should have been spiraling inward and collapsing into the nucleus. If this were the case, the atoms making up all matter would be completely unstable. Everyday experience contradicted this conclusion. Perhaps because of this problem, neither Rutherford nor anyone else paid very much attention to his new atomic model. It would take Bohr's insight to solve the problem of the Rutherford atom.

The exact timetable of when Bohr first laid eyes on Rutherford is uncertain. Both men attended the annual Cavendish dinner in December 1911. Either shortly before or shortly after, Bohr was formally introduced to Rutherford during a visit to one of his father's former students, now a physiology professor at the University of Manchester.

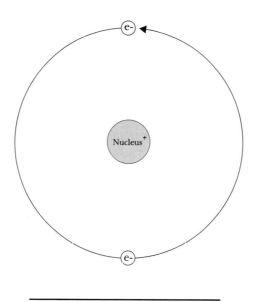

Rutherford's model of the atom proposed the existence of a positively charged nucleus containing the bulk of the particle's mass, around which the negatively charged electrons circled in rings.

Before making up his mind to transfer from Cambridge to Manchester, Bohr sought his brother's advice. After Harald's visit to Cambridge in early 1912, Niels Bohr exchanged letters with Ernest Rutherford. Years later Bohr recalled that Rutherford "said I should be welcome, but I had to settle with Thomson. He wouldn't take any student away from Thomson. . . . I just said to Thomson that I had only a year now in England and should be glad also to know something about radioactivity."[12] On his departure for Manchester in March 1912, Bohr wrote a polite note to Thomson: "I leave Cambridge with the deepest impression of your work and inspiring personality."[13]

No one would argue that industrial Manchester is a more charming university city than Cambridge. But during his four months there, Bohr lay the foundations of his greatest achievement in physics. Within two months he had put electron theory behind him forever for theoretical atomic physics. Neither Bohr nor Rutherford could have foreseen in March 1912 how Bohr's professional career would unfold. Nor could they have known how their personal ties would deepen. But Rutherford clearly took note of the young Scandinavian's arrival. He wrote an American friend on March 18, 1912, that "Bohr, a Dane, has pulled out of Cambridge and turned up here to get some experience in radioactive work."[14]

Indeed, Bohr began his time at Manchester by taking a course in experimental radioactive techniques. Just as Thomson had assigned him an experimental project, so did Rutherford. Bohr was not enthusiastic about his lab assignment in Manchester either. He continued to spend his nights working on electron theory. Bohr clearly preferred the style of his new lab director, however. He wrote Harald, "Rutherford is a man you can rely on; he comes regularly and enquires how things are going and talks about the smallest details. . . . Rutherford is such an outstanding man and really interested in the work of all the people who are around him."[15]

Bohr's work in the lab stalled after a few weeks. He had to wait for the radium he was working with to emit some "emanation"—the name Rutherford had given to the gas spontaneously given off by a radioactive substance. During that time Bohr read an article that started him thinking about the problem with the Rutherford model of the atom. By mid-June, with Rutherford's blessing, he had stopped going to the lab and devoted himself to solving the problem.

While working on his doctoral thesis, Bohr had come across new work from Germany that gave him an insight into the problem that others in the lab lacked. The new work had to do with the idea of the quantum. This was a term that physicist Max Planck had introduced in 1900. Planck calculated the amount of light that an object gives off when heated. To do so, he suggested that energy could come only in packets of certain sizes, just as one may buy six eggs or seven eggs, but not six and a half. Planck called the smallest packet of energy a quantum. The full significance of Planck's idea was not immediately understood.

Five years later, twenty-six-year-old Albert Einstein—who would become the most famous physicist of the twentieth century—used the idea of energy packets to explain the photoelectric effect. Scientists had previously discovered that when a beam of certain colors of light struck a metal, the metal released electrons, which could form an electric current. Scientists at the time assumed that light, much like sound, traveled in waves. However, they were unable to explain how light waves could result in the photoelectric effect.

Einstein argued that there were light particles, not only light waves. He suggested that light consisted of quanta (plural of quantum). Einstein's quanta were tiny packets of energy in the form of light—what people later called *photons*. Each photon behaved like a separate particle. The color of a photon depended on the amount of energy it carried. When one of these energy packets with enough energy struck a metal's atom, it forced the atom to release an electron. Another packet—say a red one instead of a blue one—might be too weak to produce the effect. Einstein would be awarded the 1921 Nobel Prize for physics for his work on the photoelectric effect.

Toward the end of his life, Bohr reflected on why he was able to figure out how Rutherford's model of the atom might really work: "I do not think that [Rutherford] really knew too much about the quantum. I think I knew much more, you see. . . . In the former years I had been very interested in the quantum."[16]

A letter to Harald on June 12 reveals how absorbed Bohr was in the problem: "I have worked out a little theory . . . which even if it is not much in itself, can perhaps shed a little light on some things concerning the structure of atoms. . . . In recent years [Rutherford] has been working out a theory of atomic structure which seems to be quite a bit more solidly based than anything we've had before. And not that my work is of the same importance or kind, yet my result does not agree so badly with his."[17]

Another letter to his brother a week later suggests Bohr's belief that he was on to something: "It could be that I've perhaps found out a little bit about the structure of atoms. . . . If I'm right, it would . . . be . . . perhaps a little piece of reality. . . . You understand that I still could be wrong, for it's not yet completely worked out (I believe it's not, however); nor do I believe that Rutherford thinks it's completely mad. . . ."[18]

Bohr knew his time in England was fast running out. He was scheduled to return to Denmark at the end of July to prepare for his August 1 wedding to Margrethe Nørlund. He was determined to write up his ideas for Rutherford before leaving. On July 22, he handed Rutherford a long memo. It presented Bohr's ideas explaining why Rutherford's model of the atom

Ernest Rutherford and Niels Bohr are seated on a bench while Mrs. Rutherford, Mrs. Oliphant, and Margrethe Bohr (left to right) relax on the lawn.

worked—why matter did not collapse in on itself. Two days later he left to get married.

By the summer of 1912, Bohr's postdoctoral year in England came to an end. His connections with Rutherford and with atomic theory did not, however. Bohr would do more than leave his mentor with a memo. He would publish three major papers in 1913 that were groundbreaking in atomic theory.

Bohr and his wife would rearrange their wedding trip to visit the Rutherfords. And from 1921, when he became director of his own scientific institute, Bohr emulated the examples set by Rutherford and his lab. Like Rutherford, he would continue with his own research while advising others. His lab, like Rutherford's, would welcome visitors from around the world. Its atmosphere would be both intense and informal. Bohr would inspire affection among those who worked with him just as Rutherford had. Many years later Bohr would say of Rutherford: "To me he had almost been like a second father."[19]

Groundbreaking Work

LATE IN LIFE, BOHR REMEMBERED THIS about his early work in atomic theory: "It was clear, and that was *the* point about the Rutherford atom, that we had something from which we could not proceed at all in any other way than by radical change."[1] The ideas that Bohr would publish after returning to Denmark would mark him as the leader of a scientific revolution. That revolution overthrew the commonsense laws that had guided physicists for several centuries.

Bohr was a champion of what became known as quantum theory. Although twenty-first-century scientists still do not completely understand the meaning of quantum theory, they rely on it as a practical tool. Bohr's work in explaining the quantum theory of atoms eventually led to electronic devices we rely on today, like computers. It also led to devices like CAT scans and MRI machines. These devices enable physicians to detect medical problems. Quantum theory lies at the foundation of modern science.

Bohr was a very cautious man in some ways. He took great pains to find the exact words to express his thoughts. He took such care not only in his lectures and publications but also in his personal letters. His speech could also be so soft that others could barely hear him. But as a scientist, he could be very fierce. When Rutherford, to whom he sent the manuscript of his 1913 papers, suggested Bohr cut the lengthy first part by one-third, Bohr made an unscheduled trip to England. He managed to convince the Nobel laureate that every section and each point had to remain. Rutherford ended up improving the English in just a few spots. He told Bohr with amusement, "I never thought you would prove so obstinate."[2]

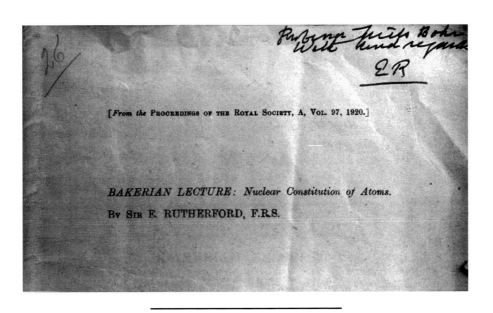

A copy of one of Rutherford's lectures stored in the Niels Bohr Archive in Copenhagen, inscribed by Rutherford to Bohr "with kind regards."

Bohr was also bold. He took risks with his theories, and often challenged long-accepted truths. German physicist Werner Heisenberg was one of Bohr's close co-workers in the 1920s. In 1968, six years after Bohr's death, he said of his former mentor: "Bohr had dared to publish ideas that later turned out to be right, even though he couldn't prove them at the time."[3] When Einstein first learned of Bohr's explanation of the atom, he said he had had similar thoughts himself, but had been afraid to publish them.

How did Bohr explain the solar system model of the atom? He did so by assuming that there were certain fixed paths in which electrons were "permitted" to move. In each of these "stationary" orbits, or levels, electrons had a precise amount of energy. Electrons would not give off energy as long as they remained in one orbit, or level. Could Bohr actually prove that there were only certain permitted paths? No, he could not. But he knew that the assumption that these paths existed worked.

Bohr assumed that an atom gained or lost energy only when an electron moved from one level to another. When an electron makes such a move, the energy is transferred in a single bundle, or quantum. This transferred energy is exactly equal to the difference between the energy of the electron in its first energy level and its final one.

In Bohr's atom, the electron can be in any of the stationary orbits but never between them. Similarly, when people climb stairs, they can rest on one step or the next, but not in between. As the heights of steps in some stairs are uneven, so too are the distances between stationary orbits and the changes in energy.

Shining light on an atom can increase its energy. If the atom gains enough energy to move one of its electrons to a higher level, the electron makes the jump. An atom with one or more electrons in higher energy levels is said to be excited. To return to its normal state, it must give off just the right amount of energy. When it jumps down to a lower level, it gives off a photon of light. When it jumps to a higher energy level, it absorbs a photon of light. The color of this light depends on the amount of energy involved in the jump.

Before Bohr, scientists already knew that a different type of atom made up each element. They also knew each element could be made to reveal a set of colors that identify it. As physicist Otto R. Frisch once explained: "Throw a little table salt (or some other sodium compound, like soda) into a gas flame, and it briefly flares yellow; a lithium compound makes it go pink, and so on. If you look at such a flame with a spectroscope (basically a glass prism with a slit in front) you don't see the usual rainbow-colored spectrum but only a few differently colored lines. . . . each kind of atom has its characteristic pattern of lines, its own 'line spectrum,' like a finger print."[4]

However, scientists did not understand why the spectrum of each element was different. Bohr explained that the electrons in each element have their own unique set of energy levels. Each element's spectrum is the energy pattern of the photons its excited atoms release. Bohr was able to explain the spectrum of the simplest of all elements, hydrogen. With a little mathematics, he calculated exactly what lines should appear. In September 1913, Albert Einstein heard of experiments proving that Bohr's explanation of the hydrogen spectrum also worked for helium. Einstein reacted with awe: "This is an enormous achievement. The theory of Bohr must then be right."[5]

Bohr's quantum model of the atom was slow to catch on, however. In the summer of 1914, he lectured on his work at the University of Göttingen in Germany. A scientist who was present at the seminar remembered the reactions: "There were people who from the beginning said, 'This is all nonsense, it is just a cheap excuse for not knowing what is going on.' Then others said that there must be something to it, and others after a rather short time just took it for the only truth, took it for granted."[6]

Eventually Bohr's work did inspire other physicists to contribute to the quantum revolution. In a September 1916 letter to Rutherford, Bohr described how popular the new field of research was becoming: "The whole field of work has indeed from a very lonely state suddenly got into a desperately crowded one where almost everybody seems hard at work."[7]

In 1922, Bohr explained why elements differ in their tendencies to form compounds. A compound is a substance that results when two or more elements join together chemically in definite amounts. Water, for example, is a compound formed when two hydrogen atoms join together chemically with one oxygen atom. Bohr related the different tendencies of elements to form compounds to the arrangement of the electrons around the nucleus.

Bohr helped to explain why each energy level in an atom can hold only a certain number of electrons. The first energy level can hold a maximum of two electrons, the second, a maximum of eight, the third, a maximum of eighteen, and so on. In some atoms, the energy level farthest from the nucleus is completely filled with electrons. Certain gases, such as helium and neon, for example, have completely filled their outermost energy levels. These gases, with eight electrons in the outermost level, do not tend to react with other elements.

Most atoms, however, do not have completely filled outer energy levels. Compounds result from the tendency of an atom to fill its outer energy level. When electrons are transferred from one atom to another or are shared, chemical bonds form.

Bohr also figured out why some elements have similar chemical properties—like forming tarnish when exposed to air. Copper and silver, for example, share that property because each has a single electron in its outermost shell. Many years later Einstein paid another compliment to Bohr for the "unique instinct" that enabled him "to discover the major laws of the spectral lines and of the electron shells of the atoms together with their significance for chemistry." Bohr's achievement, said Einstein, "appeared to me like a miracle—and appears to me as a miracle even

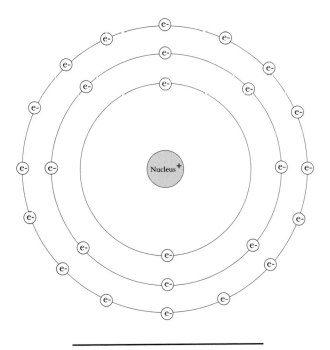

Bohr's model of the atom proposed that negatively charged electrons circled the positively charged nucleus in different levels. The first level outside the nucleus could contain a maximum of two electrons; the second level eight electrons; and the third level eighteen.

today. This is the highest form of musicality in the sphere of thought."[8]

In 1922, Bohr was awarded the Nobel Prize for physics "for his services in the investigation of the structure of atoms and of the radiation emanating from them."[9] Recipients of the award are required to deliver a lecture discussing the significance of their work. At the end of his Nobel lecture, Bohr dramatically announced the discovery of a new element, hafnium. His theory had predicted what the new element's properties would be. The discovery had been confirmed only a day earlier by two of Bohr's colleagues in Copenhagen. Hafnium provided further support for Bohr's quantum theory of the atom.

At the ceremony, the chairman of the Nobel Committee for Physics of the Royal Swedish Academy of Sciences gave the traditional "presentation speech." Toward the end of his remarks, Professor S. A. Arrhenius turned to Bohr and said, "Your great success has shown that you have found the right roads to fundamental truths, and in so doing you have laid down principles which have led to the most splendid advances, and promise abundant fruit for the work of the future."[10]

Two important contributors to that work were Werner Heisenberg and Erwin Schrödinger. In 1924, when Heisenberg was only twenty-three, he suggested that theoretical physicists should forget about trying to figure out how electrons moved inside atoms, where they could not be observed. Heisenberg proposed scientists use facts they could observe, like spectral lines, to work out mathematical descriptions of atoms. He announced one such mathematical description himself in 1925.

In 1926, Schrödinger surprised scientists by describing out an alternative mathematical description of what goes on inside the atom. In Bohr's 1913 quantum theory, electrons behaved like particles. Schrödinger based his equation on the ideas of French physicist Louis V. de Broglie. In 1924, de Broglie proposed that electrons could behave like waves. Schrödinger's wave mathematics was easier to use than Heisenberg's mathematical methods. Furthermore, Schrödinger's wave-based equation explained all the observable facts about

Werner Heisenberg (left) enjoys a meal with Niels Bohr at Bohr's institute in Copenhagen.

Bohr's theory. It also explained some facts that Bohr's theory was unable to. Over a year later, Schrödinger demonstrated that while his and Heisenberg's methods had entirely different mathematical forms, they led to exactly the same results about atomic structure and spectra. They could be used interchangeably. Schrödinger and Heisenberg's methods would change Bohr's quantum theory into a more detailed theory called *quantum mechanics*.

In 1927, Heisenberg discovered an idea

widely known as the uncertainty principle. He argued that it is impossible to know at any one instant both the location of an electron and its velocity. For example, if you shined even the weakest light beam on an electron to see where it is, you would change its velocity. Therefore, it would never be possible to predict exactly where an individual electron would be. One could say, however, where an individual electron was *likely* to be. Today's model of the atom reflects this principle. Electrons are likely to be found in cloudlike regions at different distances from the nucleus. So Bohr had been wrong to say electrons circled like planets. His model had done a great job pointing people in the right direction. But now it was replaced by a more accurate picture.

Later in 1927, Bohr developed an interpretation of quantum physics that took into account Schrödinger's and Heisenberg's contributions. Bohr argued that in quantum physics an object may behave either as a particle or as a wave, depending on the way it was studied. He insisted that a full understanding of an object's properties depended on considering both the ways it behaves like a particle and the ways it behaves like a wave. Bohr called this interpretation "the principle of complementarity." *Complementarity* is the quality exibited by two different ideas that fill each other out, or complete each other.

Bohr wanted to treat complementarity as a general principle, not just a scientific one. He believed that in most human affairs, things could only be understood by seeing the matter from two different sides, where neither side held the entire truth. (This view could be traced back to Bohr's early interests in philosophy.) While many philosophers and scientists disagreed with this view, they still usually appreciated its tolerant approach.

Albert Einstein was one of those who disagreed. Einstein regarded many of Bohr's accomplishments with wonder, pleasure, and approval—but he could not make his peace with complementarity. Einstein had been among the first to introduce the idea of the quantum. But he had always hoped to replace quantum physics

Niels Bohr chats with Albert Einstein (right) in the home of a colleague.

with another theory that better described reality. He simply could not accept a view of the world where uncertainty prevailed. As he used to say, "God does not play dice with the universe." Bohr would counter by saying, "Nor is it our business to prescribe to God how he should run the [universe]."[11]

At professional meetings over the years, Einstein would appear at breakfast and triumphantly describe a "thought experiment" that showed a flaw in Bohr's principle. (Einstein was famous for experiments carried out only in his mind.) By dinner that night, Bohr would have discovered the flaw in Einstein's reasoning. Nonetheless, by challenging Bohr, Einstein helped him refine quantum theory.

Despite their ongoing disagreement, Einstein and Bohr had deep affection for each other. Because they respected and admired each other so much, over the rest of their lives each tried—without success—to change the other's point of view.

A World-Class Institute

DESPITE THE PIONEERING WORK THAT he was involved in at that very moment, Bohr did not immediately find an appropriate position when he returned from Manchester to Copenhagen in 1912. At first he was an assistant to the sole physics professor at the University of Copenhagen, Professor Martin Knudsen. Knudsen had replaced Christian Christiansen, who had just retired. In the spring of 1914, Bohr wrote a letter to a friend explaining his employment situation: "I only have the duty of instructing the medical students in physics, and I thus have no possibility of getting pupils or assistance. . . . I am therefore working for the establishment of a teaching post in theoretical physics . . . , but there does not appear to be much hope that this will succeed."[1]

When a position opened up in Manchester at Rutherford's lab in autumn 1914, Bohr took a leave of absence from the University of Copenhagen. World War I had already broken out in August, making passage to England risky, even from neutral Denmark. The Bohrs made the sea voyage safely, however. They remained in England until early summer 1916, near the midpoint of the war. By that time the University of Copenhagen—afraid that Bohr might leave Denmark for good—had created the new position for him. Bohr was now professor of theoretical physics. It took another two years for the university to arrange to pay an assistant to relieve Bohr of the chore of teaching medical students.

In 1917, Bohr approached the university authorities. He asked them to establish a university physics institute. Once Bohr was promised his own institute, he felt an obligation to Denmark. He was sometimes tempted by offers of positions elsewhere. But Bohr never yielded to temptation, no matter how prestigious the appointment might be or how much his salary would increase.

The most tempting offer came from Britain in 1923. Bohr could have his pick of British science centers in which to work, at a salary nearly three times his current one. Since Rutherford had become director of the Cavendish a few years before, Bohr considered joining his former mentor there. When it became clear that doing so would mean a complete break with Copenhagen, he could not bring himself to leave. A few years earlier he had turned down another offer to work with Rutherford, then still in Manchester: "I feel that it is my duty here to do my best, though I feel very deeply the result will never be the same as if I could work with you."[2]

Bohr had to raise the money for his institute largely on his own. A former schoolmate collected contributions from forty private donors and twenty large firms to purchase a plot of land for the institute. The Danish government paid the salaries of a small permanent staff, including a scientific assistant, a secretary, and a trained mechanic. Over the years, Bohr applied for and received funds for equipment and the expansion of the institute's facilities. He was granted money for fellowships for visiting foreign scientists. He also received funding for the yearly conferences held at the institute, beginning in 1929. Some of the agencies that funded the institute were Danish, such as the Carlsberg Foundation, which had supported Bohr's postdoctoral year in England. Others were American, such as the Rockefeller Foundation.

The Institute for Theoretical Physics was formally opened on March 3, 1921. As it became the world's leading center for theoretical physics, Bohr became known as the "director of atomic theory." (In fact, despite the institute's name, experimental physicists worked there alongside theoreticians.) At the opening ceremonies, Bohr explained that the institute's main purpose was "To introduce a constantly renewed number of young people into the results and methods of science."[3]

A few months after the Bohrs returned to Denmark in 1916, Christian, the first of their six sons, was born. Bohr adored his sons and spent much time nurturing them, despite his busy schedule. Four of them would reach adulthood and make significant professional contributions of their own. One son, Aage, would go on to win the Nobel Prize for physics in 1975. Aage Bohr later recalled that many of the institute's young scientists became like family members: "During my early childhood, my parents lived at the Institute for Theoretical Physics (now the Niels Bohr Institute), and the remarkable generation of scientists who came to join my father in his work became for us children Uncle Kramers, Uncle Klein, Uncle Nishina, Uncle Heisenberg, Uncle Pauli, etc."[4] These names were among the most important in twentieth-century physics.

A number of these young scientists became Bohr's closest collaborators. Part of this role involved taking over the scribal chores that had once been carried out by Bohr's mother, brother, and wife. They did not merely write down what Bohr said, however, but used their own scientific gifts and insights to help him work out precisely what he wanted to say. According to one of these young men, Léon Rosenfeld from Belgium, each young physicist in Bohr's circle felt part of "a spiritual family, strongly united under Niels Bohr's paternal aegis."[5]

Helping Bohr prepare articles for publication was no easy task for these young scientists. Virtually every article Bohr wrote went through numerous drafts before he was satisfied with it. All the other scientists at the institute could keep whatever hours they liked. But Bohr's scientific assistant had to be ready to work with Bohr at any time of day or night. Watching the way Bohr worked could also be exhausting. He rarely sat still. Instead, he would pace around the room, walking faster as his thoughts became more pressing. However tired they became, his young assistants had to keep themselves alert. They had been selected for the position, after all, because of their ability to contribute to Bohr's thinking. During the years they collaborated with Bohr, it was hard for them to do their own scientific work. They did not resent the time

The exterior of the Niels Bohr Institute in Copenhagen, Denmark.

spent helping Bohr, however. They considered it a great privilege to have been chosen. They valued the experience forever as one of the greatest of their lives.

Perhaps the assistant who became closest to Bohr was Werner Heisenberg. Heisenberg was only a twenty-year-old graduate student when Bohr singled him out. Heisenberg had been confident enough to object to something Bohr said in a lecture. Afterwards, Bohr invited Heisenberg to go walking with him in the hills outside Göttingen, the German university town where Bohr had been invited to speak. During their hike, their conversation went beyond physics to philosophy. Toward the end of their discussion, Bohr invited Heisenberg to come to the institute. After Heisenberg's brief visit there in 1924, he came for several extended stays and became Bohr's assistant.

The collaboration between Bohr and Heisenberg may have been the most fruitful in the history of science. Their close relationship did not mean, however, that they never argued. In winter 1927, they were busy arguing intensely over quantum theory. Bohr had become convinced of the need to make room in quantum theory for both waves and particles. Heisenberg, meanwhile, had grown more attached to the particle view.

In mid-February, to escape the endless arguing, Bohr went off to Norway on a skiing trip. Heisenberg stayed behind to work in Copenhagen. During this period of solitary thought, each one worked out a crucial piece of quantum theory: Heisenberg's uncertainty principle and Bohr's principle of complementarity. The arguments resumed when Bohr returned. Bohr managed to reduce Heisenberg to tears over a fundamental objection to his work. Heisenberg said some hurtful things back to Bohr.

Another young scientist helped settle the argument. By late spring, Heisenberg agreed to add a few additional points to his uncertainty paper. In this postscript, Heisenberg pointed out that uncertainty in observing an electron is partly due to its dual behavior—as a particle and as a wave. That September, Bohr delivered his first public paper on complementarity at a meeting in Italy. During the discussion period, Heisenberg spoke up publicly to endorse Bohr's argument.

Just as Bohr was intimately involved with the development of Heisenberg's work, he also struggled with Erwin Schrödinger over his contribution to quantum physics. Schrödinger grew ever more convinced that it was possible to base atomic physics entirely on the wave interpretation. He was ready to abandon the idea that electrons can behave like particles.

In autumn 1926, Bohr invited Schrödinger to Copenhagen. He hoped that, face to face, he, Heisenberg, and Schrödinger could resolve their scientific differences. According to Heisenberg, "Schrödinger stayed at Bohr's house so that nothing would interrupt the conversations. . . . It is hardly possible to convey just how passionate the discussions were, how deeply rooted the convictions of each man. . . . two men were fighting for their particular interpretations of the new mathematical scheme with all the powers at their command."[6] During his visit, Schrödinger fell ill. Even while Mrs. Bohr nursed him in his sickbed, he was called upon to defend his work. He told Bohr he was close to regretting the day he took up atomic theory. Bohr responded, "But the rest of us are so grateful that you did, for you have thus brought atomic physics a decisive step forward."[7] When Schrödinger left Copenhagen after two weeks, the matter was still unresolved.

Vigorous arguments over science between Bohr and his colleagues were part of what came to be called the "Copenhagen spirit." When

Heisenberg introduced that term in 1930, he was referring to the approach to quantum theory that included the uncertainty principle and complementarity. Today this approach is usually called the "Copenhagen interpretation." The term "Copenhagen spirit" now generally refers to the type of atmosphere and style of work found at Bohr's institute.

Bohr is remembered by the scientists who worked there for allowing everyone the freedom to pursue independent research and for nurturing each one to develop an independent mind. Toward the end of his life Bohr recalled his determination to take a genuine interest in the work of all the scientists at his institute, just as Rutherford had done in Bohr's Manchester days: "I tried to be helpful all the day, you see, with anybody."[8]

Bohr's helpfulness paid off. Rutherford himself noted how Bohr's guidance had led to the development of quantum theory much more quickly than could have been predicted: "Considering the extraordinary complexity of even a single spectrum, I thought, before Bohr's

A plaque of Rutherford and a bust of Einstein on display at the Niels Bohr Institute.

contribution, that it would require centuries to get to the bottom of this complex, and yet, led by Bohr's thoughts, this was achieved in little less than a decade."[9] Many young scientists felt they had learned the most from Bohr not at lectures or seminars but while sailing, skiing, or hiking; going to Western movies; playing table tennis with him at the institute; or kicking a soccer ball around at his homes in Copenhagen and Tisvilde.

The Bohrs had bought their home in Tisvilde

in 1924. Tisvilde is about forty miles northwest of Copenhagen, close to the seashore. Bohr worked there in a small one-room cottage. The Bohrs' second son, Hans, recalled, "Many young scientists . . . also came out to Tisvilde with us in the summer, and in their intervals of their work . . . they took part in . . . games and sport."[10]

After living in an apartment on the institute grounds for about ten years, the Bohrs moved to the House of Honor on the grounds of the Carlsberg brewery in 1932. The will of the brewery's founder left the mansion as a residence to be occupied for life at no expense by the Dane whose achievements made him or her most worthy of honor. The mansion's first occupant had been Harald Høffding, Bohr's university philosophy professor and the colleague of his father. After Høffding's death in 1931, the house was prepared for the Bohrs. While they lived there it became not only a home away from home for many young scientists, but also a meeting place for distinguished foreign visitors. The Bohrs' first guests there were the Rutherfords.

One of the defining features of the Institute for Theoretical Physics was its international roster. Bohr always believed in the importance of international cooperation both in science and in politics. Even before the institute opened, Bohr envisioned it as an international center. In his application to the Carlsberg Foundation for funds to buy equipment, Bohr wrote: "It may be that in the future . . . scientists from every land will meet in Copenhagen for special studies, pursuing their common cultural ideals at the Bohr Institute for Atomic Physics."[11]

After World War I ended in November 1918, the nations that had opposed Germany in the war were slow to welcome it back into the international community. As a step in that direction, Bohr made a point of lecturing in Germany in the years immediately following the war. He met Einstein for the first time in 1920, when he gave a lecture in Berlin. He met Heisenberg for the first time in Göttingen in 1922, when he gave a series of lectures there that became known as the "Bohr festival."

Later that year, at the traditional Nobel

The Carlsberg Mansion, dubbed the House of Honor, in which Niels Bohr once lived with his family.

banquet, the new laureate spoke of the importance of international scientific cooperation: "It is especially natural for me to call to mind the emphasis on the international character of science on which Alfred Nobel's great foundation is based. This is very obvious to me, because the small contribution that I have had the good fortune to make to the development of physical science, has consisted in joining together contributions to our knowledge of nature which we owe to investigators of various nations, who have built on widely different scientific traditions."[12] Bohr then proposed a "toast to the vigorous growth of the international work on the advancement of science which is one of the high points of existence in these, in many respects, sorrowful times."[13]

Before the institute celebrated its tenth birthday, it had hosted physicists from Austria, Belgium, Canada, China, Germany, Holland, Hungary, India, Japan, Norway, Poland, Romania, Switzerland, Great Britain, the United States, and the Soviet Union. The international flavor of the institute would be modified by world events beginning in 1933, when Hitler and the Nazis came to power in Germany.

6

The Winds of War

IN 1926, BOHR AND A GROUP OF FRIENDS bought a sailboat, *Chita*. During their first sail in the summer of 1934, the weather changed unexpectedly for the worse. Christian, Bohr's oldest son, who was about to start university in the fall, was swept overboard. Bohr's sailing partners had to physically restrain the distraught father from jumping in to try to save the teenager. The boy's body was found only later in the summer.

Although Bohr was unable to save the life of his firstborn, he spent much of the 1930s working tirelessly to protect the lives of colleagues elsewhere in Europe. On January 30, 1933, Adolf Hitler became chancellor of Germany. Shortly thereafter, the Nazi regime

This photo of Christian Bohr still hangs upon the wall of the old study of Niels Bohr at the Niels Bohr Institute.

announced racial laws barring Jews from holding public positions. University professors and researchers working in German institutes were included. At least one fourth of Germany's physicists were Jewish. What would become of them?

Bohr immediately traveled to Germany. He learned how many German scientists would be affected. He sought funding for as many as possible. Bohr's institute became a temporary haven for many until permanent positions could be found for them elsewhere. Before the end of 1939, Bohr was able to get positions in Sweden,

England, or the United States for most of the Jewish refugees at the institute. (Sweden remained neutral during the war, while England and the United States were allied against Germany, Italy, and Japan.) Aware that not only physicists were affected by the Nazi laws, Bohr helped form the Danish Committee for the Support of Refugee Intellectual Workers. In addition to university staff, the committee also helped journalists, authors, and actors.

Little detailed information remains about Bohr's assistance to refugees. To keep the information from the Nazis, incriminating papers were destroyed. Individuals whom Bohr helped, however, were able to tell their stories. One of them was Otto Robert Frisch. He would go on to play a crucial role in the development of twentieth-century history. Frisch later remembered how Bohr's interest in him not only reassured Frisch's mother but also changed Frisch's life: "Bohr came to talk to me and took me by one of my waistcoat buttons and said 'You must come to Copenhagen to work with us. We like people who can actually perform thought experiments!' . . . Anyhow I felt very bucked up by Bohr's visit, his kind remark and his immensely impressive and yet benevolent face, so that I wrote to my mother 'You need no longer worry about me; God Almighty himself has taken me by my waistcoat button and spoken kindly to me.' "[1] After a number of years in Copenhagen, Frisch went on to a brilliant scientific career in England.

Because of all the young men who had flocked to Bohr's institute in the 1920s to work with him, quantum theory had been dubbed "boys' physics." With lives at stake, however, Bohr aided scientists without regard for age or gender. Physicist Hilde Levi was the last Jewish student to receive a doctorate in Berlin in the 1930s. From 1934 until she fled to Sweden in 1943, Levi worked at Bohr's institute. Like the young men who felt they were treated like members of the Bohr family, Levi was similarly welcomed by Mrs. Bohr and the children.

Beginning in 1933, Bohr did what he could to convince an older physicist to come to Copenhagen in transit to a permanent position elsewhere. This woman, Lise Meitner, happened to be Otto Frisch's aunt. Meitner, an Austrian, was able to continue working at the Kaiser Wilhelm Institute for Chemistry in Berlin until the Nazis took over Austria on March 12, 1938. The next day she was denounced as "The Jewess [who] endangers the institute."[2] (Although Meitner had converted to Christianity years earlier, she was from a Jewish family.) The following month Bohr wrote her, inviting her to the institute to give a seminar on her work on radioactivity. As important as her research was, the invitation was a pretext to get Meitner out of Germany.

Meitner was prepared to accept Bohr's offer. When she went to the Danish consulate for a travel visa, however, she could not get one. Since Austria was now officially a part of Germany, her Austrian passport was no longer valid. With her Jewish ancestry, Meitner was unlikely to get a German passport. Thanks to friends, she eventually made it safely to Sweden in August 1938. Bohr had secured an offer for her at a new institute there devoted to nuclear research.

Bohr also played a role in helping the great Italian physicist Enrico Fermi escape the clutches of Hitler's ally, Mussolini. Italy enforced racial laws later than Germany, but when it did so, those laws would have affected Fermi's family. Although Fermi himself was not Jewish, his wife, Laura, was. In autumn 1938, Fermi was visiting Bohr's institute. The identities of the Nobel laureates are usually shrouded in secrecy until the official announcement comes from Stockholm, Sweden. In this case, Bohr decided

Italian physicist Enrico Fermi. Uranium experiments begun by Fermi would become instrumental in unlocking the secrets of atomic power.

to deviate from custom. He told Fermi he would shortly be awarded the Nobel Prize. Armed with this knowledge, Fermi did just as Bohr had hoped he would: He took his entire family to the Nobel Prize ceremonies in Sweden. After a brief stop in Copenhagen, they left for New York. Fermi had previously arranged a position there at Columbia University.

Meanwhile, research at Bohr's institute had shifted focus. In the 1920s the institute had been a main center of quantum theory. In the 1930s it became just as active in the field of nuclear physics—the study of the behavior and structure of the atomic nucleus. Bohr applied for and received grants from agencies, including the Rockefeller Foundation and the Carlsberg Foundation, for the large and expensive equipment needed to carry out nuclear research.

More surprisingly, the Institute for Theoretical Physics also became a center of experimental biology. Bohr took advantage of funds the Rockefeller Foundation earmarked for senior European scholars who had lost their positions. In 1934, he brought over to the institute an old friend from his postdoctoral days in Manchester—the Hungarian-Jewish aristocrat George de Hevesy. Hevesy, trained as a physicist, had been teaching physical chemistry in Freiburg, Germany. At Bohr's institute, Hevesy went on to pioneer the use of radioactivity in biological research. Hilde Levi and Otto Frisch designed the equipment Hevesy needed for his earliest work.

In 1936, Bohr used insights he had gained more than twenty-five years earlier, while researching surface tension, to improve on his model of the atom. In an article published that year, he compared the nucleus of an atom to a drop of liquid. A force like surface tension was what held the nucleus together. Waves of energy were reflected back and forth within the "drop." These waves explained the transfer of energy from place to place within the nucleus. This liquid-drop model would play a pivotal role in a discovery Otto Frisch and his aunt, Lise Meitner, would make toward the end of 1938.

Frisch and Meitner had developed the custom of spending the Christmas holiday together. In December 1938, Frisch left

Copenhagen to meet Meitner in a small town in Sweden. On their first morning together, Meitner began discussing some puzzling results of experiments conducted by German chemist Otto Hahn, her former colleague. Hahn had kept in touch with Meitner after she fled Germany. Together with Fritz Strassmann, Hahn was carrying out experiments that Meitner had helped plan. These experiments involved bombarding uranium with neutrons. (Neutrons are tiny atomic particles with no electric charge. They had been discovered in 1932 by James Chadwick in England.)

Meitner and Hahn—along with other physicists—had been experimenting with uranium for several years. These experiments were first begun by Enrico Fermi in 1934. By bombarding uranium with neutrons, scientists had originally expected to create a new element that was heavier than uranium. The outcome was different, however. Their experiments were resulting in the formation of lighter elements than they had anticipated. No one could explain this outcome.

Now Frisch, on cross-country skis, and Meitner, keeping up with him on foot, interrupted their excursion through the Swedish woods. Using Bohr's liquid drop model of the nucleus, Meitner and Frisch figured out that the uranium nucleus could actually split into two nuclei that are lighter. Pulling out some scraps of paper and a pencil, they did some calculations. According to Einstein's famous law, $E=mc^2$, that tiny difference in mass (m) between the nuclei should result in the release of a huge amount of energy (E).

Frisch and Meitner knew they had discovered something extremely important. As soon as Frisch returned to Copenhagen, he went to see Bohr. Frisch later described his brief meeting with the busy institute director: "I had hardly begun to tell him when he smote his forehead with his hand and exclaimed: 'Oh what idiots we all have been! Oh but this is wonderful! This is just as it must be!'"[3] Bohr encouraged Frisch to submit a paper explaining their work as soon as possible.

In long-distance calls between Stockholm and Copenhagen, aunt and nephew wrote a short paper. In it, Frisch compared the splitting nucleus to the way organisms divide. He asked an American biologist working with Hevesy what the name of the biological process was. The answer was "fission." Frisch's choice of the name "nuclear fission" stuck.

Frisch came to see Bohr just as the latter was preparing to leave for several months in the United States. There, Bohr spent much of his time working with a young American physicist, John A. Wheeler. Bohr worked with Wheeler in much the same way he had worked with Heisenberg and others in the 1920s. The earlier collaborations had helped define quantum theory. Now the Bohr-Wheeler collaboration provided the details of nuclear fission.

When a uranium nucleus is split by neutrons, tremendous energy is released, as well as other neutrons. These neutrons can go on to split other atoms. This process is called a chain reaction. Bohr realized that fission could take place in a rare form of uranium, U-235, but not in the more common form, U-238. In the same paper, Bohr and Wheeler showed how the nuclear chain reaction could be controlled.

As scientists in the United States hastened to do experiments that confirmed the European work, they began to think what fission might mean. If enough U-235 could be collected, could a chain reaction be started that would release large amounts of energy? Such energy could be used to produce a weapon unlike any humankind had ever experienced before.

Bohr did not think a bomb was likely to be developed any time soon. He thought it would be very difficult to separate U-235 from U-238. But Otto Frisch, now in England, calculated that it would be possible to separate enough to make a bomb. He and many others feared what would happen if Hitler's scientists were the first to develop an atomic bomb. Before long, government projects to develop an atomic bomb were under way in both Britain and the United States.

World War II officially broke out on September 1, 1939. In April 1940, the German army occupied Denmark with ease. Bohr refused to collaborate with the Nazi authorities. He immediately destroyed records on the refugee

Fission

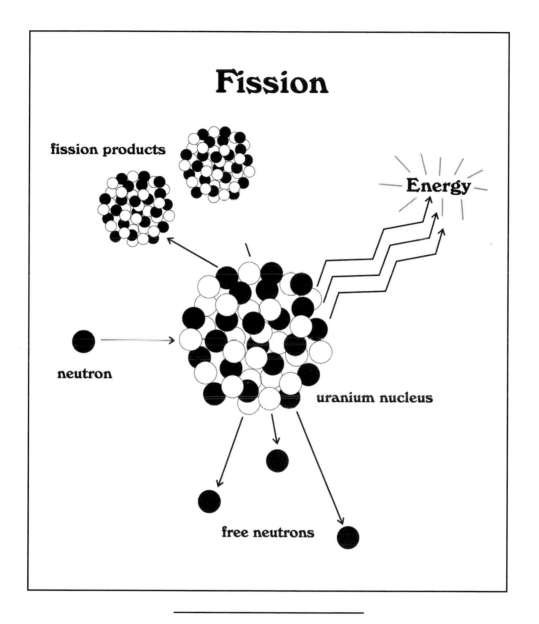

fission products

Energy

neutron

uranium nucleus

free neutrons

When a neutron splits the nucleus of a U-235 atom, two smaller fragments result, as well as "free neutrons" that may go on to split the nuclei of other atoms in a chain reaction. Energy is also released.

scientists he had brought to Copenhagen. He developed close ties with the Danish resistance. He urged the government to resist strongly if the Nazis tried to impose racial laws on Denmark.

It became ever more dangerous for foreign visitors to stay on at Bohr's institute. The last foreign scientist left in November 1940. Depleted of its international staff, research activity at the institute declined. Bohr was now also cut off from research developments in other countries.

Toward the end of Bohr's 1939 visit to the United States, friends begged him to stay. But he insisted on returning to Denmark. He knew his failure to return would have a negative effect on Danish morale. Immediately after the Germans occupied Denmark, Bohr was again offered positions in the United States. He refused them all. As a sign of his commitment to Denmark, he spent a great deal of effort writing the introduction to a volume, *Denmark's Culture in the Year 1940*. In it he quoted one of the world's great story-tellers, Danish author Hans Christian Andersen: "In Denmark I was born; there I have my home: there I have roots; from there my world proceeds."[4] When the volume appeared the following year, it helped restore Danish pride and hope.

Trying to keep the institute going despite the Nazi occupation was difficult for Bohr. Perhaps one of the most distressing experiences of this time came in September 1941. It involved a visit from his old friend, Werner Heisenberg. Heisenberg had been much more than a close collaborator of Bohr's. They had been nearly as close as father and son. Other non-Jewish German intellectuals had left Nazi Germany. Heisenberg, however, had chosen to remain. He was now scientific director of nuclear fission research for the German army.

What exactly happened during the visit is unclear. Neither man made a written report at the time. They held their conversation outdoors to avoid indoor bugging devices. What is known is that the visit outraged Bohr. He believed Heisenberg's goal was to gather information on the efforts in America and Britain to build fission weapons, or atomic bombs.

After the war, Heisenberg told people that his

moral objections to the bomb kept him from developing one. He claimed he was trying, through Bohr, to send a message to American and British physicists that they, too, should give up the deadly project. Heisenberg's postwar self-justifications angered Bohr. The relationship between the two men, once so close, would never be the same.

In the 1990s, British playwright Michael Frayn wrote a play called *Copenhagen*. It is about Heisenberg's mysterious visit. In it, Frayn explored several possibilities of what Heisenberg might have told or tried to tell Bohr. In March 2000, at a New York symposium about Frayn's play, the public learned that Bohr wrote an angry letter to Heisenberg after the war. This letter was never mailed, however. The Bohr family originally intended to release the letter in 2012, fifty years after Bohr's death. But because there was so much public interest in it, the family released it in 2002, along with several other related documents.

The letter is undated but was probably written in 1957. In it, Bohr remembered that during the 1941 visit, Heisenberg gave him "the firm impression" that, with Heisenberg as the leader of the effort, "everything was being done in Germany to develop atomic weapons." According to Bohr, Heisenberg also said that he had no need to discuss any details with Bohr, since he had "spent the past two years working more or less exclusively on such preparations." In the newly released documents, Bohr also revealed that Heisenberg told him during the visit of his "conviction that the war, if it lasted sufficiently long, would be decided with atomic weapons."[5]

In early 1943, the Danish resistance delivered Chadwick's message hidden in a pair of keys. Bohr turned down this invitation to join British scientists. He understood the British sought his help in developing atomic weapons. He continued to believe that it would be too hard to collect enough U-235 to develop a bomb. If it were possible at all, he imagined it would take a very long time. Still, when rumors reached Copenhagen about increased uranium processing in Germany, Bohr passed on the information to Chadwick.

At the end of September 1943, Bohr understood that the time had come for him and his family to leave Denmark. He learned from the Swedish ambassador in Copenhagen that the Germans were preparing to rid Denmark of its Jewish population. He and his brother—both sons of a Jewish mother—might be arrested at any moment. That very night, with the aid of the Danish resistance, Bohr and his wife crossed the Sound, the narrow channel separating Denmark and Sweden. Their sons followed soon after.

Once in Sweden, Bohr immediately began efforts to help Denmark's 7,000 Jews. He hoped the Swedish government might convince the Nazis to reroute the Danish Jews to Sweden instead of to concentration camps. The Nazis dismissed Sweden's suggestion as unjustified meddling in German affairs. Because of Bohr's request, however, the Swedish government announced over the radio that Sweden was ready to receive the Danish Jews. Danish Jews in hiding took heart. One recalled: "At the pastor's house I heard on the Swedish radio that the Bohr brothers had fled to Sweden by boat and that the Danish Jews were being cordially received."[6]

The Danish resistance now began the dangerous task of smuggling Danish Jews across the Sound. Thanks to Bohr, the Swedish police along the coast stopped interrogating refugees met by Swedish boats. If information about the escape route reached the wrong ears, the consequences might be dreadful. In the end, almost 6,000 Danish Jews arrived safely in Sweden. Fewer than 500 were sent to concentration camps.

Although Mrs. Bohr and three Bohr sons spent the rest of the war in Sweden, Bohr himself stayed only a week. His presence there was a hazard. The Germans knew where he was. He was guarded by Danish officers and Swedish police.

In early October, Bohr made a three-hour flight to Britain in the bomb bay of a Mosquito, a small bomber plane. The aircraft was not pressurized. The pilot knew Bohr would have to use oxygen when they reached a height of 30,000 feet. The helmet holding Bohr's earphones was too small for his large head, however. Bohr never heard the pilot's orders, and he fainted. The two-man crew in the cockpit worried when Bohr did not confirm the request to put on his oxygen mask. Luckily, by the time the Mosquito landed in Scotland, Bohr had regained consciousness. He suffered no lasting harm.

Bohr's son Aage was now a twenty-one-year-old university graduate with a degree in physics. A second Mosquito carried Aage safely to Britain. Safe transport in a mosquito could not be taken for granted, however. Just after the Bohrs' flights, the crew and passenger of another Mosquito lost their lives.

Father and son would spend the remaining months of the war in Britain and the United States. At the request of the British, Bohr involved himself in official efforts to prepare bombs for wartime use. He also began his own efforts to stop a postwar arms race.

An Open World

WHEN BOHR ARRIVED IN ENGLAND IN October 1943, he was amazed to learn just how far American and British scientists had advanced in developing the bomb. He had been convinced that nuclear science could not be put to military use anytime soon. Now Bohr learned that the U.S. government had recently opened a laboratory in Los Alamos, New Mexico. In that isolated spot, the final preparations for the first two atomic bombs were to be made. The British were sending some scientists to Los Alamos to help with the work, which was called the Manhattan Project. They believed Bohr's presence on the British team would increase its influence.

Bohr and his son Aage arrived at Los Alamos in early 1944. The entire project was shrouded in secrecy. Never mind the fact that Bohr's suitcase was clearly personalized with his name in big, black letters. The Bohrs had been assigned code names: Nicholas and James Baker. At Los Alamos, they became Uncle Nick and Jim.

When Bohr said goodbye to his wife in Sweden, he was forbidden to tell her just where he was going and why. All he was permitted to say was that he was working on postwar scientific cooperation. The explanation was only partial, but it was not far from the truth. Bohr made only a small contribution to the development of the first atomic bombs. He helped design a device to start the chain reaction in one of the Los Alamos bombs. Bohr spent much of his time in England and the United States trying to convince people of the importance of international cooperation, starting immediately.

Bohr was one of the first to understand that the atomic bomb presented the world not only with a terrible threat but with a great opportunity to improve international relations. The scientists at Los Alamos may have been the first to hear his ideas. All of them had been convinced that their work was crucial. It was important that Hitler not be the first to develop atomic weapons. (The Allies did not learn until after the war that the German army decided in late 1941 to de-emphasize its fission project in favor of developing rockets and jet aircraft.)

As their work came closer to producing actual bombs, some scientists began to worry. They understood how deadly such weapons would be. Otto Frisch, who had given nuclear fission its name, recalled: "Many of us were beginning to worry about what the future might hold for a humanity in possession of such a dreadful weapon, and once again it was Bohr who taught us to think constructively and hopefully about that situation."[1]

J. Robert Oppenheimer, the director of Los Alamos, also remembered Bohr's reassuring role. Bohr encouraged the Los Alamos team to believe that "the cooperation which he had experienced among scientists would play a helpful part" in bringing about a good outcome from the project.[2] Bohr expressed his hope that this terrible weapon would put an end to major war. If nations understood that the whole world stood to lose if such weapons were used, perhaps they would agree to ban them.

Bohr had been particularly convinced that an arms race could be prevented only if the United States told the Soviet Union about the bomb before the weapon was used. He believed that all nations should freely exchange their scientific information. He also believed that governments should open their laboratories and their military installations to outside inspection. Bohr understood that scientists everywhere had the same abilities. He felt it was foolhardy to believe that a scientific achievement mastered in one country would not soon be matched elsewhere.

Bohr took his message to U. S. President Franklin D. Roosevelt and to British Prime Minister Winston Churchill. He approached the president through Supreme Court Justice Felix Frankfurter, whom Bohr had met in 1933. At

A photo of one of the atomic bombs developed at Los Alamos. Bohr helped design a device to start the chain reaction in one of the bombs.

that time both had been concerned about helping German refugees.

Through Frankfurter, Bohr was told the president wanted atomic energy used peacefully, not destructively. Roosevelt delegated Bohr to speak with Churchill about how the two nations might approach the matter. With great difficulty, a meeting was set up in May 1944 between Bohr and Churchill. It went very badly. The prime minister entered in a bad mood and left in a worse mood. He was not interested in Bohr's point of view. At the end of the short interview, Bohr asked Churchill if he might send him a letter summarizing his views. Churchill responded that he would always be happy to hear from the professor—but not about political issues.

Bohr's meeting with Roosevelt in late August 1944 was more promising. The president spoke with Bohr for more than an hour. He appeared to be in tune with what Bohr was saying. He chuckled when he heard Bohr's description of his meeting with Churchill. The president told Bohr he was to meet with Churchill in September and would be sure to take the matter up with him then. He would get back to Bohr afterwards.

Bohr's hopes were soon dashed, however. Churchill and Roosevelt met in September 1944 at the Roosevelt home in Hyde Park, New York. There they agreed to keep information about the nuclear weapons project secret. On his return to

England, Churchill also expressed his suspicions of Bohr: "It seems to me Bohr ought to be confined or at any rate made to see that he is very near the edge of mortal crimes." A memo summarizing the agreement concluded by the two leaders at Hyde Park includes the following warning: "Enquiries should be made regarding the activities of Professor Bohr and steps taken to ensure that he is responsible for no leakage of information."[3] Advisors who knew Bohr assured both Churchill and Roosevelt that such fears were misguided. Nothing became of the suggestion that Bohr be kept under suspicion or arrested.

President Roosevelt died on April 12, 1945. Frankfurter heard the news as he was concluding a talk with the British ambassador on how they could promote Bohr's ideas. At the time of his death, the president was working on a speech that reflected those ideas: "Today we are faced with the preeminent fact that if civilization is to survive, we must cultivate the science of human relationships—the ability to all people of all kinds to live together and work together in the same world, at peace."[4]

Early the next month, the war ended in Europe. In August, Bohr and his wife were reunited in England after nearly two years apart. A shadow was cast over their joyful reunion, however. On August 6, the United States dropped one of the Los Alamos bombs on Hiroshima, Japan. Three days later, a second bomb was dropped on Nagasaki. The bombs accounted for more than 100,000 deaths. But without the bombs, the U.S. would have been forced to mount an invasion of Japan, and even more lives could have been lost.

On August 11, *The Times* of London published Bohr's first public appeal for "an open world." In it he argued that if civilization was to continue, nations would have to change the way they conducted themselves. "The issue centers on world wide cooperation to prevent any use of the new sources of energy which does not serve mankind as a whole."[5]

On August 25, the Bohrs returned to Copenhagen. A little over a week later, Japan surrendered. World War II was finally over.

By 1949, the Soviet Union had mastered

nuclear technology. Each side hurried to be the first to develop the next destructive weapon. A "cold war" broke out between the "Eastern bloc" of Communist countries, led by the Soviet Union, and the "Western bloc" of non-Communist countries, led by the United States. (The rivalry between the two sides began to diminish only in the 1980s. Soviet leader Mikhail Gorbachev then instituted a policy of openness—a reminder of what Bohr had sought.)

Bohr never gave up his hope of increasing international cooperation. In June 1950, he sent an open letter to the United Nations. He called for free exchange of information among nations. He envisioned "an open world where each nation can assert itself solely by the extent to which it can contribute to the common culture."[6] Little attention was paid to Bohr's plea. Before the end of the month, one of the bloodiest wars of the century broke out. The Korean War lasted over three years. Millions of lives were disrupted. Atomic weapons were not used, however.

Bohr did not succeed in preventing an arms

A bust of Bohr on display at the Niels Bohr Institute.

race. In the 1950s, however, he succeeded in furthering international scientific exchange. He helped establish three scientific research centers: CERN, Nordita, and Risø. The name CERN comes from the initials for the French words meaning "European Council for Nuclear Research." One of the reasons for starting a European research lab was to woo back some of the scientists who had left Europe for the United States in the 1930s. Between 1952 and 1957, the

CERN theoretical physics group was based at Bohr's institute in Copenhagen. Located near Geneva, Switzerland, CERN today is the world's largest research center for the study of subatomic particles. Today, CERN's membership includes twenty European countries and several observer states.

Some scientists had felt that the natural location for CERN would be Bohr's institute. Others had objected, and they had their way. But in early 1953, scientists from three Scandinavian countries—Denmark, Norway, and Sweden began discussing the establishment of a joint theoretical physics institute alongside Bohr's institute. The new institute, Nordita, opened its doors in September 1957. Its full name is the Nordic Institute for Theoretical Physics. By 1956, Nordita included Finland and Iceland as members. Although the institute is funded by those five Scandinavian countries, the institute's permanent staff includes scientists from other countries. Modeling itself on Bohr's institute, Nordita has always invited foreign visitors for stays of varying lengths.

Of the international physics centers Bohr helped found, CERN represents the broad European community, and Nordita represents the countries of northern Europe. Risø, the last of these centers, began as a purely Danish research institute. Over the years, it has become increasingly more international. Bohr was determined to find ways in which nuclear energy could be put to peaceful uses. The Danish government established the Danish Atomic Energy Commission to investigate such uses. In December 1955, Bohr was chosen to head it.

Bohr personally chose the spot on the Risø peninsula (about twenty miles west of Copenhagen) where a national energy laboratory would be built. The Risø research center opened in 1958. By the time Bohr died four years later, other countries had asked for its advice on energy issues. Bohr was pleased by the international contacts that resulted from research conducted there. Today Risø has expanded its research interests beyond energy to such fields as health, physics, and information technology.

Another satisfaction of Bohr's last years came

in October 1957. The United States selected Bohr as the winner of the first Atoms for Peace Award. The award noted Bohr's contributions in unlocking "many of Nature's . . . secrets." It described his Institute for Theoretical Physics as "an intellectual and spiritual center for scientists." It cited Bohr's "great moral force in behalf of the utilization of atomic energy for peaceful purposes."[7]

A little over five years later, in June 1962, Bohr and his wife were in Germany for a gathering of Nobel laureates. While there, Bohr suffered a minor stroke. He was flown back to Copenhagen, where he was hospitalized. When he was released, he and his wife went to their summer home. In August the Bohrs celebrated their fiftieth wedding anniversary in the company of their children and grandchildren. By autumn, he was ready to resume his busy schedule.

On Saturday, November 17, Bohr completed the first of a planned series of interviews on the history of quantum physics. Throughout the interviews, he spoke about discussing things with the interviewers in the future. Just three days earlier, he had said, "I will try to clear my thoughts another day."[8] That day never came. After lunch on Sunday, November 18, Bohr retired to his room for a nap. Moments later he called out his wife's name. She found him on the floor next to the bed, unconscious. The medical diagnosis was death due to heart failure.

At the time, Bohr's institute was planning to hold a conference in 1963. It was meant to celebrate the 50th anniversary of Bohr's first papers on quantum theory. Instead, the conference was held as a memorial. Two years later, on what would have been Bohr's eightieth birthday, the Institute for Theoretical Physics in Copenhagen was renamed the Niels Bohr Institute. Twenty years later, in 1985, the International Commission of

A 500 Kroner bill, bearing the likeness of Niels Bohr.

Physics Education commemorated the 100th anniversary of Bohr's birth by publishing a book in his honor. The book consists of essays about Bohr. Many of the essays echo the same theme: that Bohr was more than a great scientist—he was also a great human being.

In the words of one of the essayists: "Nothing has done more to convince me that there once existed friends of mankind with the human wisdom of Confucius and Buddha, Jesus and Pericles, Erasmus and Lincoln than walks and talks under the beech trees of Klampenborg Forest with Niels Bohr."[9]

Activities

Activity One: Surface Tension

In 1905, Niels Bohr conducted a prize-winning experiment involving the surface tension of water. Surface tension is what makes the surface of a liquid act like stretched elastic. This activity is meant to demonstrate surface tension.

Materials needed:

A transparent cup or container

Water

A small straight pin

Procedure:

Fill the cup or container with water. Hold the pin horizontal to the water and let it drop. (The idea is to not let the point of the needle touch the water surface.) **Please do <u>not</u> perform this activity unless a teacher or parent is present and watching. Always be careful when handling pins or other sharp objects.** If the pin should sink, try placing it slowly on the surface of the water. Keep trying until it successfully stays afloat atop the water. Now, take the pin out and drop it into the water so that its point strikes the water first. It should then sink to the bottom of the container.

Surface tension occurs as a result of cohesion—the force of attraction between the molecules of a substance. Cohesion is what holds a substance together. Solids are very cohesive, liquids are mildly cohesive, and gases are almost completely noncohesive. In your container, the water molecules that are below the surface are attracted to other molecules in all directions. But the molecules at the surface are attracted only to the other molecules below and to the side. This creates a constant pull on the surface molecules that results in surface tension. The pin will sink

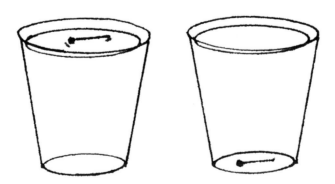

only when it punctures this surface. When it fails to puncture it, the surface tension holds it afloat.

Now dip your fingers into the container. Flick some of the water onto your arm or a tabletop. The water should form as tiny spheres or "beads." It does so because surface tension will pull uncontained water into the shape with the smallest possible surface area: a sphere. This fact explains why rain falls in the form of tiny drops. This concept of surface tension later helped Niels Bohr conceive of his liquid-drop model of the atom.

Activity Two: Electron Shells

A typical atom possesses both protons and neutrons in its nucleus, with electrons orbiting outside it. In 1913, Niels Bohr proposed that electrons orbit the nucleus in orbits of fixed sizes. Later on, scientists came to consider that the electrons are found in shells, the thick surfaces of spheres. As a result of Bohr's model, electrons are never found between shells. The first shell can hold a maximum of two electrons; the second shell, a maximum of eight; the third a maximum of eighteen, and so on. The outermost shell of an atom is called the valence shell. The number of electrons in the valence shell determines how reactive an element is. If an atom's valence shell is completely filled with electrons, it will not react with other atoms. If an atom's valence shell is not filled, it will be quicker to react with other atoms.

For example, hydrogen has an atomic number of one. This means a hydrogen atom has one proton and one electron. Since the first shell of an atom can hold up to two electrons, there is room in a hydrogen atom to add an electron. (Because it has only one electron, the hydrogen atom's first shell is its valence shell.) This makes hydrogen very reactive. It can form chemical bonds easily. Helium has an atomic number of two. This means a helium atom has two protons and two electrons. Like hydrogen, a helium atom's first shell is its valence shell. Since the first shell can only hold two electrons, there is no room in a helium atom to add an electron. For this reason, helium does not react with other elements.

Elements with more than two electrons in their atoms begin to fill out a second shell. Lithium has an atomic number of three. This means a lithium atom has three protons and three electrons. The first shell holds two electrons and the second shell—the atom's valence shell—holds one. Since the second shell can hold up to eight electrons, a lithium atom has room to add up to seven more electrons to its valence shell. As a result, lithium is very reactive.

This activity involves constructing models of the valence shells of different atoms.

Materials needed:

A bag of gumdrops

Toothpicks

A box of donuts

Procedure:

In this activity each donut will represent the valence shell of an atom. The gumdrops will represent electrons. As you know, a lithium atom possesses one electron in its valence shell. To create a model of the atom's valence shell, stick a toothpick in one gumdrop. Now attach the other end of the toothpick to the donut, as illustrated below:

You have just created a model of the valence shell of a lithium atom! (The donut represents only the middle portion of the sphere that is the shell. The top and bottom of the shell do not appear in this demonstration.) Boron has an atomic number of five, so it has three electrons in its valence shell. Add two more gumdrops and you will have made a model of the valence shell of a boron atom. See if you can make models of valence shells of other atoms with the following atomic numbers:

4–beryllium   7–nitrogen   9–fluorine

6–carbon   8–oxygen   10–neon

Question:

Can you tell which of these elements would be unreactive?

Carbon dioxide is a common gas in our atmosphere. It is the gas we breathe out when we exhale. It is also the gas that plants need in order to survive and grow. Chemically, the formation of carbon dioxide is a simple reaction, involving one carbon atom and two oxygen atoms. Take three donuts and construct one valence shell of a carbon atom and two valence shells of oxygen atoms, as shown:

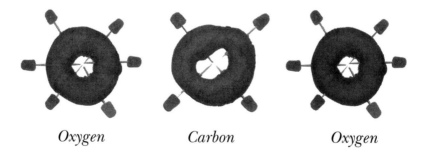

Oxygen   *Carbon*   *Oxygen*

Can you see how the three atoms form their chemical bond? Each valence shell of oxygen has room for two more electrons. Carbon has four electrons in its valence shell. Take two of carbon's electrons and use it to fill out one of the oxygen shells. Take the remaining two carbon electrons and fill out the other oxygen shell. This is how carbon reacts with oxygen to form carbon dioxide.

Two atoms of hydrogen and one atom of oxygen create water. Can you determine how the reaction between these atoms takes place by making models with your donuts and gumdrops?

Other reactions are more complicated because they require many more atoms than just three. Which of the other atoms you've constructed do you think would tend to react with others? If you like, you can look up other elements and make more models. Elements with atomic numbers greater than ten involve the third valence shell, which can hold up to eighteen electrons—you may need to buy a few more bags of gumdrops to make models of those shells!

Chronology

1885—Niels Henrik David Bohr born in Copenhagen, Denmark, on October 7.

1903—Bohr begins studying physics at the University of Copenhagen.

1907—Bohr receives the gold medal of the Royal Danish Academy of Sciences and Letters for a prize essay on the surface tension of water.

1909—Bohr receives his master's degree from the University of Copenhagen.

1911—Bohr receives his doctorate on the electron theory of metals. He travels to England for a year of postdoctoral research.

1912—Bohr marries Margrethe Nørlund.

1913—Bohr presents his quantum theory of the hydrogen atom.

1914—World War I breaks out. Bohr accepts a two-year appointment at the University of Manchester, England.

1916—Bohr becomes a professor of theoretical physics at the University of Copenhagen.

1921—The Institute for Theoretical Physics in Copenhagen opens.

1922—Bohr publishes his quantum theory of chemistry. He receives the Nobel Prize "for his investigations of the structure of atoms and of the radiation emanating from them."

1927—Bohr introduces the complementarity concept.

1931—Bohr, as Denmark's most distinguished citizen, is awarded the House of Honor in Copenhagen.

1933—Bohr helps support scientists fired from German universities because of Nazi laws.

1936—Bohr develops his model of the atomic nucleus.

1939—Bohr explains uranium fission (together with John A. Wheeler). World War II begins.

1940—German troops occupy Denmark.

1943—Bohr and his wife flee Denmark.

1943–1945—Bohr is associated with American and British atomic weapons projects.

1945—Bohr returns to Denmark several months after German forces surrender.

1950—Bohr sends an "Open Letter" to the United Nations.

1952—The theory division of CERN starts work

in Copenhagen, with Bohr as its first director.

1957—Nordita starts operations in Copenhagen, with Bohr as the first director of its board. Bohr receives the first Atoms for Peace award. Bohr writes a letter to Heisenberg but never mails it.

1958—Bohr formally opens the Risø research center.

1962—Bohr dies on November 18 at his home in Copenhagen.

1965—The Institute for Theoretical Physics in Copenhagen is renamed the Niels Bohr Institute to commemorate what would have been Bohr's eightieth birthday.

2002—The Niels Bohr Archive in Copenhagen releases several documents related to Heisenberg's visit to Bohr in 1941.

Chapter Notes

Chapter 1. A Secret Message
1. Margaret Gowing, "Niels Bohr and Nuclear Weapons," *Niels Bohr: A Centenary Volume*, ed. A. P. French and P. J. Kennedy (Cambridge, Mass.: Harvard University Press, 1985), p. 268.

2. Niels Blaedel, *Harmony and Unity: The Life of Niels Bohr* (Madison, Wis.: Science Tech Publishers, 1988), p. 214.

Chapter 2. Growing Up in Denmark
1. Ruth Moore, *Niels Bohr: The Man, His Science, & the World They Changed* (New York: Knopf, 1966), p. 14.

2. Niels Bohr, "Determination of the Surface Tension of Water by the Method of Jet Vibration," *Philosophical Transactions of the Royal Society of London, 1909, Series A, Containing Papers of a Mathematical or Physical Character* vol. 209, pp. 281–317.

3. Abraham Pais, *Niels Bohr's Times, in Physics, Philosophy, and Polity* (Oxford: Clarendon Press, 1991), p. 108.

4. Niels Bohr, *Collected Works* (Amsterdam: North-Holland Publishing Company, 1972), vol. 1, p. 295.

5. Ruth Moore, *Niels Bohr: The Man, His Science, & the World They Changed* (New York: Knopf, 1966), p. 29.

Chapter 3. Postdoctoral Work in England
1. John L. Heilbron, *Historical Studies in the Theory of Atomic Structure* (New York: Arno Press, 1981), p. 66.

2. León Rosenfield and Erik Rüdinger, "The Decisive Years," *Niels Bohr: His Life and Work as Seen by His Friends and Colleagues*, ed. Stefan Rozental (New York: John Wiley & Sons, Inc., 1967), p. 40.

3. Ibid., p. 40.

4. Ibid., p. 41.

5. Niels Bohr, interview by Thomas Kuhn, November 1, 1962, pp. 6–7. Archives for the History of Quantum Physics, Niels Bohr Library, American Institute of Physics, College Park, Md., USA.

6. J. J. Thomson, "Bakerian Lecture: Rays of Positive Electricity," *Proceedings of the Royal Society of London, Series A, Containing Papers of a Mathematical and Physical Character*, vol. 89, no. 607, August 1, 1913, pp. 1–20.

7. Niels Bohr, interview by Thomas Kuhn, p. 7.

8. Ibid., p. 7.

9. Ibid., p. 8–9.

10. Ibid., p. 7.

11. Abraham Pais, *Niels Bohr's Times, in Physics, Philosophy, and Polity* Oxford: Claredon Press, 1991, p. 122.

12. Niels Bohr, interview by Thomas Kuhn, p. 8.

13. Pais, p. 125.

14. Richard Rhodes, *The Making of the Atomic Bomb* (New York: Simon and Schuster, 1986), p. 52.

15. *Niels Bohr: His Life and Work as Seen by His Friends and Colleagues*, Rosenfeld and Rüdinger, p. 46.

16. Niels Bohr, interview by Thomas Kuhn, p. 5.

17. David Wilson, *Rutherford: Simple Genius* (Cambridge, Mass.: MIT Press, 1983), p. 327.

18. Heilbron, p. 238.

19. Abraham Pais, *The Genius of Science: A Portrait Gallery of Twentieth-Century Physicists* (Oxford: Oxford University Press, 2000), p. 18.

Chapter 4. Groundbreaking Work

1. Richard Rhodes, *The Making of the Atomic Bomb* (New York: Simon and Schuster, 1986), p. 77.

2. Ruth Moore, *Niels Bohr: The Man, His Science, & the World They Changed* (New York: Knopf, 1966), p. 62.

3. Karl von Meyenn and Engelbert Schucking, "Wolfgang Pauli," *Physics Today*, February 2001, p. 44.

4. Otto R. Frisch, *What Little I Remember* (New York: Cambridge University Press, 1979), p. 22.

5. Abraham Pais, *Niels Bohr's Times, in Physics, Philosophy, and Polity* (Oxford: Claredon Press, 1991), p. 154.

6. Ibid., p. 155.

7. Ibid., p. 161.

8. Ibid., p. 179.

9. "The Nobel Prize in Physics 1922," *The Official Web Site of the Nobel Foundation*, June 16, 2000, <http://www.nobel.se/physics/laureates/1922/> (August 8, 2001).

10. "Presentation Speech by Professor S. A. Arrhenius, Chairman of the Nobel Committee for Physics of the Royal Swedish Academy of Sciences," *The Official Web Site of the Nobel Foundation*, June 16, 2000, <http://www.nobel.se/physics/laureates/1922/press.html> (August 8, 2001).

11. Werner Heisenberg, "Reminiscences from 1926 and 1927," *Niels Bohr: A Centenary Volume*, ed. A. P. French and P. J. Kennedy (Cambridge, Mass.: Harvard University Press, 1985), p. 171.

Chapter 5. A World-Class Institute

1. Niels Blaedel, *Harmony and Unity: The Life of Niels Bohr* (Madison, Wis.: Science Tech Publishers, 1988), p. 67.

2. Ruth Moore, "Niels Bohr as a Political Figure,"

Niels Bohr: A Centenary Volume, ed. A. P. French and P. J. Kennedy (Cambridge, Mass.: Harvard University Press, 1985), p. 254.

3. Abraham Pais, *The Genius of Science: A Portrait Gallery of Twentieth-Century Physicists* (Oxford: Oxford University Press, 2000), p. 20.

4. Official Web Site of the Nobel Foundation, n.d., <http://www.nobel.se/physics/laureates/1975/bohr-autobio.html> (August 8, 2001).

5. Finn Aaserud, *Redirecting Science: Niels Bohr: Philanthropy, and the Rise of Nuclear Physics* (Cambridge, England: Cambridge University Press, 1990), p. 11.

6. Werner Heisenberg, "Reminiscences from 1926 and 1927," *Niels Bohr: A Centenary Volume*, ed. A. P. French and P. J. Kennedy (Cambridge, Mass.: Harvard University Press, 1985), p. 164.

7. Richard Rhodes, *The Making of the Atomic Bomb* (New York: Simon and Schuster, 1986), p. 129.

8. Niels Bohr, interview by Thomas Kuhn, November 1, 1962, Archives for the History of Quantum Physics, Niels Bohr Library, American Institute of Physics, College Park, Md., USA.

9. Blaedel, p. 119.

10. Abraham Pais, *Niels Bohr's Times, in Physics, Philosophy, and Polity* (Oxford: Clarendon Press, 1991), p. 249.

11. Blaedel, p. 71.

12. Ibid., p. 100.

13. Abraham Pais, *The Genius of Science: A Portrait Gallery of Twentieth-Century Physicists* (Oxford: Oxford University Press, 2000), p. 21.

Chapter 6. The Winds of War

1. Otto R. Frisch, *What Little I Remember* (New York: Cambridge University Press, 1979), p. 76.

2. Ruth Lewin Sime, *Lise Meitner: A Life in Physics* (Berkeley, Calif.: University of California Press, 1996), p. 184.

3. Frisch, p. 116.

4. Niels Blaedel, *Harmony and Unity: The Life of Niels Bohr* (Madison, Wis.: Science Tech Publishers, 1988), p. 213.

5. Niels Bohr, as quoted by James Glanz, "New Light Shed on Role of Chief of Nazi Atom Project," *The New York Times,* February 7, 2002, p. A12.

6. Richard Rhodes, *The Making of the Atomic Bomb* (New York: Simon and Schuster, 1986), p. 484.

Chapter 7. An Open World

1. Ruth Moore, *Niels Bohr: The Man, His Science, & the World They Changed* (New York: Knopf, 1966), p. 330.

2. Richard Rhodes, *The Making of the Atomic Bomb* (New York: Simon and Schuster, 1986), p. 524.

3. Moore, pp. 352–353.

4. Ibid., p. 363.

5. Ibid., p. 379.

6. Abraham Pais, *Niels Bohr's Times, in Physics, Philosophy, and Polity* (Oxford: Clarendon Press, 1991), p. 517.

7. Ibid., p. 2.

8. Niels Bohr, interview by Thomas Kuhn, November 1, 1962, Archives for the History of Quantum Physics, Niels Bohr Library, American Institute of Physics, College Park, Md., USA.

9. John A. Wheeler, "Physics in Copenhagen in 1934 and 1935," *Niels Bohr: A Centenary Volume,* ed. A. P. French and P. J. Kennedy (Cambridge, Mass.: Harvard University Press, 1985), p. 226.

Glossary

atom—Smallest bit of an element that has all the properties of that element.

chain reaction—Reaction that, once started, keeps itself going, as one individual reaction causes adjacent ones to occur.

cohesion—Molecular attraction that unites the particles of a body throughout its mass.

complementarity—The relationship between two different ideas (or people or things) that fill out, or complement, one another.

complementarity principle—In quantum theory, the principle that both wave and particle behavior must be considered to understand atoms.

"Copenhagen interpretation"—The interpretation of quantum theory that includes the principles of complementarity and uncertainty.

"Copenhagen spirit"—The intense but informal atmosphere that prevailed at Bohr's Institute for Theoretical Physics in Copenhagen.

electron—Negatively charged particle orbiting the nucleus of an atom.

electron shell—A fixed path at a specific distance from the nucleus of an atom in which an orbiting electron does not give off energy. Each electron shell can hold no more than a certain number of electrons.

electron theory of metals—The theory that the motion of electrons in metals accounts for their properties.

element—Any of the simplest substances of matter that cannot be decomposed by heat, light, or electricity.

energy level—One of the possible amounts of energy an electron may have in an atom, according to quantum theory.

fission—The process of splitting heavy nuclei into lighter fragments, resulting in the release of energy.

line spectrum—Characteristic pattern of light and color given off (or taken up) by an element's atoms as they release (or absorb) energy.

Nazis—Members of German political party that governed Germany from 1933 to the end of World War II.

neutron—Particle having no electric charge, found either by itself or in a nucleus.

Nobel prize—Prestigious award founded in 1901 for outstanding achievement in physics, chemistry, physiology or medicine, literature, and world peace. A sixth prize, for economic sciences, was added in 1969.

nuclear energy—Energy that is released when mass is transformed into energy, for example, as atoms undergo fission.

nucleus—Positively charged core of an atom.

photoelectric effect—The ejection of electrons from the surface of a metal plate when light particles with enough energy fall on it.

photon—A quantum of light energy.

proton—Positively charged particles found free or in a nucleus.

quantum—Small packet of energy.

quantum theory—Scientific theory that describes the structure of the atom and the motion of atomic particles. It also explains how atoms absorb and give off energy as light and why elements share certain chemical properties.

radioactivity—Spontaneous decay of a nucleus into a lighter nucleus, very tiny particles, and radiation.

surface tension—Property of a liquid that makes its surface act as if it were a stretched elastic sheet.

uncertainty principle—Principle that certain pairs of quantities, such as the position and velocity of a particle, cannot be measured with exactness at the same time.

valence shell—An atom's outermost electron shell.

Further Reading

Fox, Karen. *The Chain Reaction: Pioneers of Nuclear Science*. Danbury, Conn.: Franklin Watts, Inc., 1998.

Goldenstern, Joyce. *Albert Einstein: Physicist and Genius*. Berkeley Heights, N.J.: Enslow Publishers, Inc., 1995.

Hamilton, Janet. *Lise Meitner: Pioneer of Nuclear Fission*. Berkeley Heights, N.J.: Enslow Publishers, Inc., 2002.

Spangenburg, Ray and Diane K. Moser, *Niels Bohr: Gentle Genius of Denmark*. New York: Facts on File, 1995.

Internet Addresses

Niels Bohr Institute (NBI)
http://www.nbi.dk/Welcome.html

Bohr Mini-Exhibit
http://www.aip.org/history/esva/exhibits/bohr.htm

Niels Henrik David Bohr
http://www-groups.dcs.st-and.ac.uk/~history/
    Mathematicians/Bohr_Niels.html

Index